MIKAELA SHIFFRIN

SPORTS SUPERSTARS

BY GOLRIZ GOLKAR

BELLWETHER MEDIA • MINNEAPOLIS, MN

Torque brims with excitement perfect for thrill-seekers of all kinds. Discover daring survival skills, explore uncharted worlds, and marvel at mighty engines and extreme sports. In *Torque* books, anything can happen. Are you ready?

This edition first published in 2026 by Bellwether Media, Inc.

No part of this publication may be reproduced in whole or in part without written permission of the publisher. For information regarding permission, write to Bellwether Media, Inc., Attention: Permissions Department, 3500 American Blvd W, Suite 150, Bloomington, MN 55431.

Library of Congress Cataloging-in-Publication Data

LC record for Mikaela Shiffrin available at: https://lccn.loc.gov/2025013874

Text copyright © 2026 by Bellwether Media, Inc. TORQUE and associated logos are trademarks and/or registered trademarks of Bellwether Media, Inc. Bellwether Media is a division of FlutterBee Education Group.

Editor: Kieran Downs   Designer: Gabriel Hilger

Printed in the United States of America, North Mankato, MN.

TABLE OF CONTENTS

SKIING TO VICTORY 4
WHO IS MIKAELA SHIFFRIN? 6
A RISING STAR 8
A SKIING SUPERSTAR 12
SHIFFRIN'S FUTURE 20
GLOSSARY 22
TO LEARN MORE 23
INDEX 24

SKIING TO VICTORY

It is the 2014 Sochi **Winter Olympics**. The second run of the women's **slalom** is starting. Mikaela Shiffrin kicks out of the start. She speeds through the gates. She almost falls! But she stays on her skis.

The crowd cheers as she crosses the finish line. Shiffrin finishes with the fastest time. She wins the gold medal!

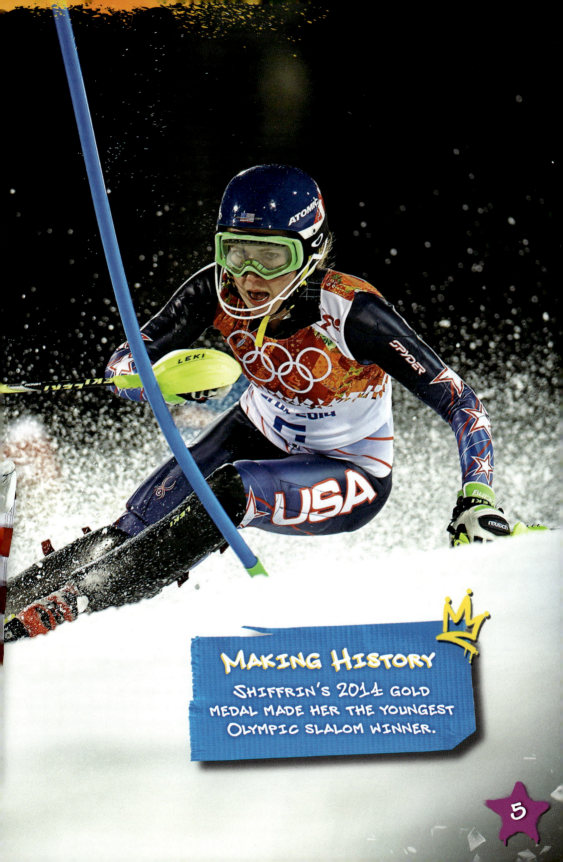

Making History
Shiffrin's 2014 gold medal made her the youngest Olympic slalom winner.

WHO IS MIKAELA SHIFFRIN?

Mikaela Shiffrin is one of the top alpine skiers of all time. She has won several Olympic medals. Shiffrin has more **FIS Ski World Cup** wins than any other alpine skier.

MIKAELA SHIFFRIN

BIRTHDAY March 13, 1995

HOMETOWN Vail, Colorado

EVENTS slalom, giant slalom, super-G, downhill, combined, and parallel slalom

HEIGHT 5 feet 7 inches

JOINED U.S. Ski and Snowboard in 2011

Shiffrin also works with companies. Some of them help the earth. Others help people make healthy choices. She also supports **charities** that help people in need.

A RISING STAR

Shiffrin's parents taught her to ski from a young age. By age 8, she was racing with a youth ski club.

SHIFFRIN AND HER PARENTS

Shiffrin skied better and faster than most kids in her club. She went to a private school with a skiing program at age 11. She trained hard there.

Shiffrin started winning major events at age 15. She won four races at different **NorAm Cup** events over two months.

Shiffrin won a bronze medal in slalom at the 2011 **Junior World Ski Championships**. She won a bronze medal in slalom. She also won gold in slalom at the **U.S. Alpine National Championships** that year. She became the youngest American alpine skier to win a national championship.

2011 JUNIOR WORLD SKI CHAMPIONSHIPS

FAVORITES

FOOD	SPORT OTHER THAN SKIING	ANIMAL	VACATION SPOT
pasta	tennis	horse	Maui

2011 U.S. ALPINE NATIONAL CHAMPIONSHIPS

CALM DOWN
Shiffrin calms her nerves before a race by doing a word search.

11

A SKIING SUPERSTAR

Shiffrin found success quickly. In 2012, she won her first World Cup slalom race. Shiffrin then won the World Cup slalom title for the 2012–2013 season. In 2013, she won the slalom at the FIS Alpine World Championships.

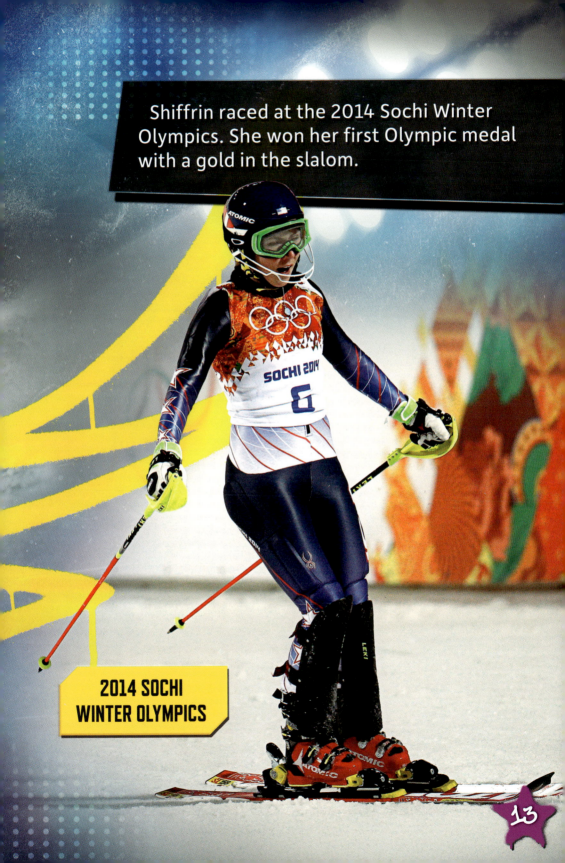

Shiffrin raced at the 2014 Sochi Winter Olympics. She won her first Olympic medal with a gold in the slalom.

2014 SOCHI WINTER OLYMPICS

Shiffrin continued to win World Cup events. She became the slalom champion again in the 2013–2014 and 2014–2015 seasons. She also won her first World Cup **giant slalom** race.

Shiffrin won the slalom events at the 2015 and 2017 World Championships. In the 2016–2017 season, she won the World Cup slalom and overall titles.

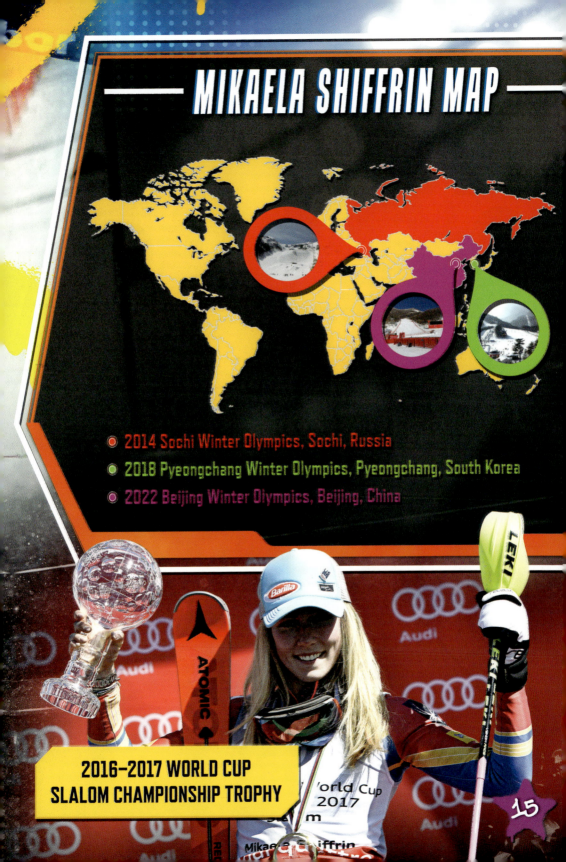

Shiffrin won gold in the giant slalom at the 2018 Pyeongchang Winter Olympics. She won the World Cup slalom and overall titles in the 2017–2018 season.

In 2018–2019, Shiffrin was the overall, **super-G**, giant slalom, and slalom champion. She won two gold medals at the 2019 World Championships.

2018 PYEONGCHANG WINTER OLYMPICS

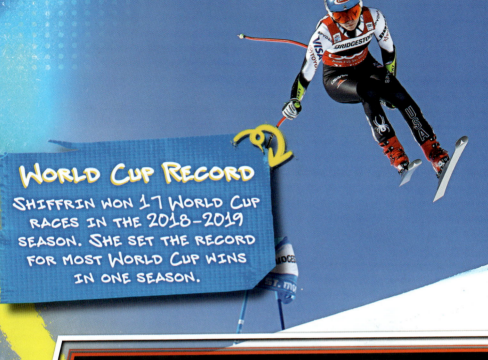

World Cup Record

Shiffrin won 17 World Cup races in the 2018-2019 season. She set the record for most World Cup wins in one season.

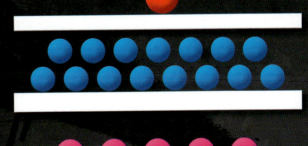

TROPHY SHELF

2 Olympic gold medals

1 Olympic silver medal

15 World Championship medals

5-time FIS Ski World Cup overall champion

In 2020, Shiffrin's father passed away. Shiffrin took a break from skiing. She skied in the 2022 Beijing Winter Olympics. But she left with no medals.

Shiffrin won the World Cup overall title in 2022. In 2023, she broke the record for most World Cup race wins. She also won her fifth overall title. In 2024, she won her eighth slalom title.

2022 BEIJING WINTER OLYMPICS

TIMELINE

— **2011** —
Shiffrin wins a gold medal in slalom at the U.S. Alpine National Championships

— **2012** —
Shiffrin wins her first World Cup race

— **2013** —
Shiffrin wins the slalom event at the World Championships

100 Wins
In 2025, Shiffrin won her 100th World Cup Race!

— 2014 —
Shiffrin wins her first Olympic gold medal at the Sochi Winter Olympics

— 2018 —
Shiffrin wins a gold and a silver medal at the Pyeongchang Winter Olympics

— 2023 —
Shiffrin sets the new world record for most World Cup race wins

SHIFFRIN'S FUTURE

Shiffrin helps charities that give youth access to sports. In late 2024, Shiffrin began working with the Share Winter **Foundation**. She works to make skiing more accessible for kids across the country.

Shiffrin hopes to win more races. She plans to ski at the 2026 Winter Olympics. On and off the ski slopes, she is a champion!

GLOSSARY

charities—organizations that help people in need

FIS Ski World Cup—an international series of ski races; FIS stands for International Ski and Snowboard Federation.

foundation—an organization that helps people and communities

giant slalom—a ski race that is on a longer and steeper course than a slalom

Junior World Ski Championships—an annual ski competition for top youth skiers aged 16 to 20 from all over the world

NorAm Cup—an annual ski competition in North America organized by the International Ski Federation in which winners may advance to Ski World Cup competitions

slalom—a ski race where skiers make several quick turns around gates

super-G—a ski race where skiers race down a long, steep course with long turns

U.S. Alpine National Championships—an annual ski competition organized by U.S. Ski & Snowboard to decide the best skier in the U.S.

Winter Olympics—a worldwide winter sports contest held in a different country every four years

TO LEARN MORE

AT THE LIBRARY

Bolte, Mari. *Mikaela Shiffrin: Olympic Skiing Legend.* North Mankato, Minn.: Capstone Press, 2024.

Gish, Ashley. *Alpine Skiing.* Mankato, Minn.: Creative Education Paperbacks, 2026.

Tischler, Joe. *Mikaela Shiffrin.* Mankato, Minn.: Amicus Publishing, 2025.

ON THE WEB

Factsurfer.com gives you a safe, fun way to find more information.

1. Go to www.factsurfer.com

2. Enter "Mikaela Shiffrin" into the search box and click 🔍.

3. Select your book cover to see a list of related content.

INDEX

awards, 4, 5, 6, 10, 13, 15, 16
charities, 7, 20
childhood, 8, 9, 10
family, 8, 18
favorites, 11
FIS Alpine World Championships, 12, 14, 16
FIS Ski World Cup, 6, 12, 14, 15, 16, 17, 18, 19
giant slalom, 14, 16
Junior World Ski Championships, 10
map, 15
NorAm Cup, 10
profile, 7
record, 5, 10, 17, 18, 19
Share Winter Foundation, 20
slalom, 4, 5, 10, 12, 13, 14, 16, 18
super-G, 16
timeline, 18–19
trophy shelf, 17
U.S. Alpine National Championships, 10, 11
Winter Olympics, 4, 5, 6, 13, 16, 18, 21
word search, 11

The images in this book are reproduced through the courtesy of: Frank Gunn/ The Canadian Press/ AP Images, front cover; Christophe Pallot/ Agence Zoom/ Stringer/ Getty Images, pp. 3, 17; Alexander Hassenstein/ Staff/ Getty Images, pp. 4, 8; Simon Bruty/ Contributor/ Getty Images, p. 5; dpa picture alliance/ Alamy Stock Photo, p. 6; Christian Bruna/ Stringer/ Getty Images, p. 7 (Mikaela Shiffrin); TT News Agency/ Alamy Stock Photo, p. 9; Anthony Anex/ AP Images, p. 10; timolina, p. 11 (pasta); New Africa, p. 11 (tennis); Kseniya Abramova, p. 11 (horse); shanemyersphoto, p. 11 (Maui); Nathan Bilow/ AP Images, p. 11 (Mikaela Shiffrin); Alain Grosclaude/ Agence Zoom/ Stringer/ Getty Images, p. 12; Christophe Ena/ AP Images, p. 13; Pacific Press/ Contributor/ Getty Images, p. 14; Sergei Kazantsev/ Wikipedia, p. 15 (2014 Sochi Winter Olympics); Kate McLoughlin/ Wikipedia, p. 15 (2018 Pyeongchang Winter Olympics); ATR1992/ Wikipedia, p. 15 (2022 Beijing Winter Olympics); Francis Bompard/ Agence Zoom/ Stringer/ Getty Images, p. 15 (2016–2017 World Cup Slalom championship trophy); Erick W. Rasco/ Contributor/ Getty Images, p. 16; DIMITAR DILKOFF/ Contributor/ Getty Images, p. 18 (2022 Beijing Winter Olympics); Action Plus Sports Images/ Alamy Stock Photo, p. 18 (2013); PONTUS LUNDAHL/ Contributor/ Getty Images, p. 19; Grinchenkova Anzhela, p. 19 (2014 gold medal); FLORIAN CHOBLET/ Contributor/ Getty Images, p. 19 (2018); Klaus Pressberger/ Contributor/ Getty Images, p. 20; Sean M. Haffey/ Staff/ Getty Images, p. 21; APA-PictureDesk/ Alamy Stock Photo, p. 23.